FARMING WITH ANIMALS

Written by Charis Mather

Library of Congress Control Number:
The Library of Congress Control Number is available on the Library of Congress website.

ISBN
979-8-89359-425-6 (library bound)
979-8-89359-445-4 (paperback)
979-8-89359-484-3 (epub)
979-8-89359-465-2 (hosted ebook)

Printed in the United States of America
Mankato, MN
012026

sales@northstareditions.com
888-417-0195

Written by:
Charis Mather

Edited by:
Noah Leatherland

Designed by:
Ker Ker Lee

Image Credits – Images courtesy of Shutterstock.com, unless otherwise stated.

Cover & Recurring – Biscotto Design, Ysami, Hybrid_Graphics, Belozersky, yusufdemirci, Lexi Claus, WinWinFolly, Gold Power. 4–5 – Visionsi, WildlifeWorld. 6–7 – Paul Knowles, Eric Buermeyer, Peter Klampfer, Tohuwabohu 1976, Leonid Sorokin. 8–9 – Baloncici, Vladimir Kovrizhnik. 10–11 – monticello. 12–13 – New Africa, znmysteryPhoto, Marina Demeshko. 14–15 – Ratthaphong Ekariyasap, Juice Verve. 16–17 – Simon Collins, mark reinstein. 18–19 – Dusan Petkovic, Caftor. 20–21 – Mai.Chayakorn, Vinnikava Viktoryia. 22–23 – Lucian Coman, FabrikaSimf.

CONTENTS

Words that look like this can be found in the glossary on page 24.

FARMING IS FASCINATING

Every year, billions of animals are farmed. Animals are farmed for food and other products. Animal farming takes hard work all year round.

Farmers who work with animals have a responsibility. They must care for animals. They need to provide animals with clean and healthy living spaces. Animal farming is a fascinating job.

ALL KINDS OF HOMES

Farm animals have different needs, so they have different kinds of homes.

Ranches and Pastures

Ranches and pastures are large, open areas of land. They have plenty of space for grazing.

Coops

Coops are warm places for chickens to lay eggs. Coops also keep them safe from predators.

Barns, Sheds, and Shelters

Barns, sheds, and shelters protect animals when bad weather hits.

Beehives

Large numbers of bees stay in wooden beehives. They have young here and protect their queens.

Net Pens

Fish are often farmed in underwater areas called net pens. Sometimes young fish are raised in smaller pens called hatcheries.

A YEAR ON AN ANIMAL FARM

Each season, animal farmers have different jobs to do. In spring, farmers help with the births of animals. They give extra care to the babies and their mothers.

In the summer, farmers separate the young animals from their mothers. The young learn to feed themselves.

In autumn, farmers start breeding their animals.

During winter, farmers keep their animals warm and fed.

WHAT ARE ANIMALS FARMED FOR?

Many animals are farmed for food.

Meat

COMES FROM: MANY KINDS OF ANIMALS

Pork, chicken, beef, lamb, goat, fish, and other seafoods are some of the most popular types of meat.

Dairy

COMES FROM: COWS, SHEEP, GOATS, CAMELS, AND BUFFALO

Dairy includes milk and foods made with milk, such as cheese, butter, and yogurt.

Honey

COMES FROM: HONEYBEES

Honeybees collect nectar from flowers. They turn it into sweet honey. Farmers collect honey from beehives.

Eggs

COME FROM: CHICKENS, DUCKS, AND OTHER BIRDS

Some birds lay eggs that are sold for food.

Some animals are farmed for non-food products.

Materials

Wool

COMES FROM: SHEEP

Wool can be turned into yarn. Yarn can be used to make clothes.

Leather

COMES FROM: MANY KINDS OF ANIMALS

Leather comes from animal skin. It is used for making products such as clothes and bags.

Other Products

Beeswax

COMES FROM: HONEYBEES

Beeswax is used for making candles. Honeybees make it after eating honey. They use beeswax to build their hives.

Beauty Products

COME FROM: MANY KINDS OF ANIMALS

Lots of beauty products use animal parts such as fat, bones, and shells.

SPECIAL EQUIPMENT

Farmers use many kinds of equipment to collect animal products.

Farmers collect wool from their sheep with shears or electric clippers.

Shearing is painless for sheep.

Some dairy farmers collect milk by hand. Big farms usually use machines. Farmers are responsible for keeping the machines clean. This keeps the animals healthy and the milk safe to drink.

LOOKING AFTER THE LAND

Unfortunately, animal farming can be damaging to the environment. Sometimes land is cleared of plants to make room for farm animals. This can be bad for the wild animals that cannot live there anymore.

Animals can also add damaging gases into the air, such as methane. Cows make a lot of methane. The more cows there are, the more methane collects in the air.

The environment needs a balance of gases. Too much animal farming unbalances it.

ANIMAL WELFARE

Many farm animals end up going to slaughter. But it's still important that farmers treat their animals well while they are alive. This is called animal welfare.

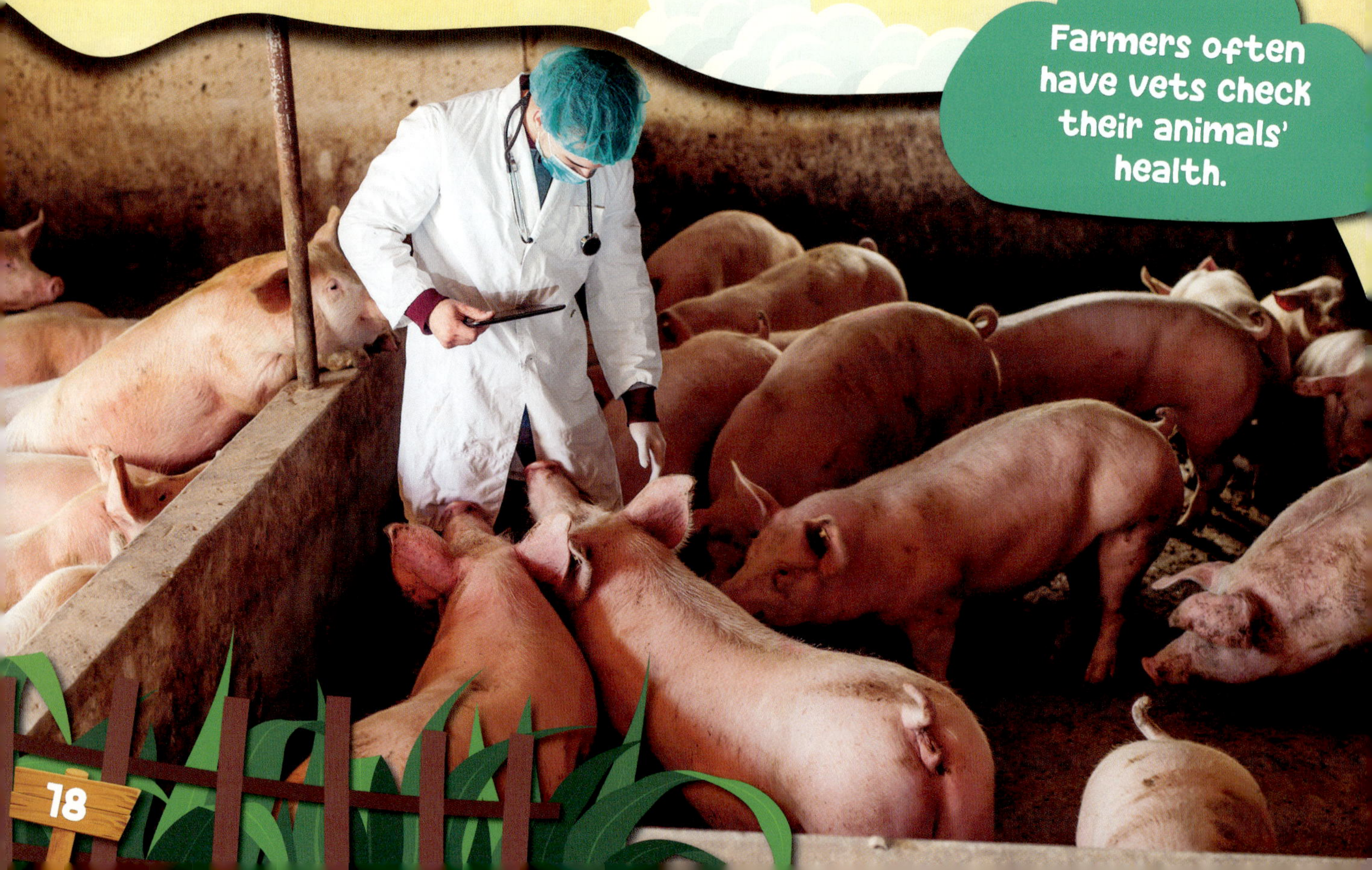

Farmers often have vets check their animals' health.

Animals shouldn't feel pain or fear. They shouldn't live in dirty, crowded areas. They should have healthy food, clean water, and plenty of space. Farmers must care for their needs.

WHAT'S WRONG WITH ANIMAL FARMING?

Many farms do not provide proper animal welfare. These farms keep too many animals in small indoor areas. They feed animals cheap, unhealthy food. This is known as factory farming.

It is easy for factory farms to spread diseases.

Many people disagree with animal farming because of how animals can be treated. Some people think that keeping animals just to slaughter them is wrong, even if they are treated well on farms.

People who choose not to eat or use animal products are called vegans.

THE PART PEOPLE PLAY

Around the world, billions of people depend on animal farming to live. Many people get their food and clothing from the animals that farmers work so hard to look after.

People should learn and understand where animal products come from. This way, people can make sure that farmers treat animals and the environment well all around the world.

GLOSSARY

breeding getting animals to have young together

environment the natural world

gases things that are like air, which fill any space available

grazing eating grass in a field

nectar a sweet liquid made by plants

predators animals that hunt other animals for food

products things that are made to be used or sold

responsibility something you have to do or are in charge of doing

slaughter to kill an animal for food

INDEX